Peter Handley

A film libretto

All Told.

#1.

The Saturday Poem.

Poetry never paid the rent did it.

Your words don't clean the toilet floor

or lift the grime from underneath the cooker.

Show me a rhyming couplet that swiped

away the cobwebs from behind the tv set.

When was the last time you punctuated

the staircase or drove an exclamation mark

into that light bulb that needs changing in the living

room?

But the point is, none of this would exist

without the cleaner having the courage

to put out the idea and keep living it.

Yer know what thought did.

As Che stands there while the rain begins

listening to a recitation with the washing in hand

And the whole world, slowly revolving around

a full stop.

All Told.

#2.

In Tilbury near Cambridge.

At Asda in Tilbury, Essex, England.

One steps through a dog end fag~ butted footbath

by the electronic sliding doors into a vaped haze

decompression chamber.

Here the multi~ national grocer must take note

in an on~time~food~chain~management kind of way

the difference between instrumentation and orchestration.

How cauliflowers ploughed back into the land economy

or wonky vegetables, take a day off from the vegetative

nature of patriarchy.

The vernacular spelt like bread with common sense,

just off the roundabout from Windrush Avenue and

Colonial Way

by the Amazon Fulfilment Centre and

Old Mother Thames, the slag.

Like the old whore society lifting her skirt and leaving a

terrible stink.

Where wishes are hatched and dispatched in quartered

twenty four hour shifts

and practical life matters arrive by public bus or private

transport.

Pawelski clocks on in pink fluorescence, through his

minimum waged turnstile.

And to consolidate Group Think this morning's internal

government news update

reminds civil servants of twelve things to agree upon

about poverty

that point number seven insists the average distance below
the poverty line

has been shrinking according to The World Bank matrix
used,

fer the telling.

The metre of cluster evidence is Stanley, the dilly dallying
retiree

safeguarding his chivalrous behaviour by not burning the
baked beans

in a bleached out restaurant among the hapless clamour of
ignorance -

He rarely sees the light beyond the light reflected.

Intelligence is overrated, spastick, over there,

by the pet food aisle

where Naturo the holistic grain free food for digestive and
allergy sensitive dogs is availed.

A young black girl in a pink tutu, angel wings strapped to her back

is heading excitedly towards Mr Kipling's Unicorn Slices

sold for the price of a fat white boys ransome in re-fined sugars.

Disgarded english country apples and a browning organic banana skin, half consumed

in a plastic tray of plastic cherry coca-collared bottles. Please recycle.

Here we are then fetid moss growing in damp velcro.

If only magpies could shop.

Nirvana would be here by the inclined travellating check - out

especially for the diss abled, confuses the capable –

A shell suited european truck driver stacking up on

Lithuanian cheap meats

and a cornucopia of Polish pig carcasses for the long

journey home.

God and nature re-assemble in the car park

by the mother and baby slots.

The scoliosed high visibility employee pushing baskets to

the click and collect.

One final hurricane spin scrubber, by JBL, to deliver

to the backside of a heavily financed blue Mercedes.

Amidst the detritus of empty pizza boxes seagulls, on a

Thames river sabbatical

vie with the ravens from Hangman's Wood, scavenging

for tit bits.

In stores now, subject to availability.

Save money, live better.

Pawelski, the migrant, on a limited lunch break from his

shift in the Fulfilment Centre

is arrested by two community police officers in the

summer outdoor barbecue section of the gardening aisle

and convicted later of arson by an immoderate local

magistrate.

The big bold motivational messages strapped across the

walls in his staff canteen read

Are right. A Lot, have backbone, disagree and commit,

invent and simplify.

Bias for action. Ownership. Insist on the Highest

Standards, Customer Obsession

dive deep, think big, hire and deliver the best, deliver

results, earn trust

of others. Frugality.

The souls of dimeloquent dead and dieing slaves shop

in Tilbury.

All Told.

#3.

In Cambridge near Tilbury.

Where some of the finest minds

across the Generations of the World

come to purchase their freekeh grains

and ponder the Weetabix for cerebral breakfasts.

Where the front of The Telegraph,

recently £1.60, tells us that

the sex abuse of girls in schools is rife

in the knowing that this academic town underfunds

the resource for rectification in a

nationalleaguetableof things, by a golden mile.

And all the lovely check-out ladies

have all their pHd's

in macro-economics and thermo-nuclear knitting

primed, for the doing.

Where personal noise pollution is misconstrued

as piped car-park music, there's no mistaking

Mahler's 4th, a recent manuscript of which

just sold at Sotheby's for four an narf million quid.

Georgette is ready to tell herstory

for Christian Aid confessional charity begettings

because 'she just needs someone to listen', innit.

The polite pervasive perfume of privilege

where even the soup in the café is vibrant

the children recite pye with their burgers

to thirty seven decimal places 3.1415926585 bla blah

blah…

and more fries and nuggets and nobody really

knows there's a war on in Bradford Doncaster

Gravesend and The Yemen.

Such is the luxury of global academic shopping.

Back on the estate style of things

the early morning atmosphere has frozen

the flags of The Jack and The George

hung on lamp posts above the communal

christ mass trimmings saying –

'Nothing changes, nothing's changed'.

We've only to order the charente chocolate torsades

from the harried and acned café assistant to know

that life is researched and complete, almost wretched.

'I don't think I'm a miserable cow.

 I'm justifiably irritated'.

She said.

All Told.

#4.

Very Little Helps.

He passed on, 'the fifteenth of last month

just before the Wolf Moon hit it's sell by date

stretching a sigh along the Madrid fault line unnoticed.

I'd have to check with my loyalty points

but I'm pretty certain by the bar-code recognition;

at the super-market it was. All the milk half sour

in the incandescent daze of the dairy aisles

a complication with the refrigeration unit,

the Manager said in a press release published

after verification from a higher authority

at Head-Office, to ensure unbreastfed babies

wouldn't be sueing the company, for compensation.

They're smart, those little bastards, and getting smarter,

don't stop issuing the plastic bags, he was heard to say

under breath re-cycled from the air-con units,

som nam bew list ically

I'm sixty three and a bit, it's how I'd like

to be remembered, he said.

He wore new shoes, that was always a sign of progress,

functionality, he said.

No need to say anymore, leaving a conversation

as a man leaves footwear in a closet

in a house he means to return to.

I was with him when he gave-up disgusted,

a fortunate event to be there in the milk aisle,

reminiscing on gold-tops

and staring on at row by row of creme-fraiche

doing rarefied eastern meditation practices

by the skimmed milk,

we absorbed each other's consciousness

by the low fat yoghurt, and laughed.

Before the check-out we were happy as the cows

that come home in the advertisemeants.

There was a bright white light and neither of us

were quite sure if the flourescent refrigeration units,

pulsing away to keep the salt free butter hard

were choking on it's own cholesterol,

but anyhow

it didn't matter much, how could it.

The purity and clarity in those eyes, the bliss in goodbye,

There, in the moment as the sirloin stacked

in the meat counter

ensured a connection with that other.

Helping you spend less, every day.

All Told.

#5.

More Reasons.

Matured, we communicate through ailment

through what ails

and fear.

The black flower says 'Blessed am I', upon the earth

before we rape our selves show us more compassion

before we rape ourselves of empathy.

Every word that told a story

every lie that became myth, eventually

we thought we knew truth was the lesser of two evils

and God writes straight on crooked lines.

You forgot the acute disseminated encephalitis

you don't have, have we all,

even take a government prick for it.

It will be your dimensional ecology they'll say

and you will be ok with that, with that,

for now.

It's a frickin' letdown mate, a frickin' letdown,

you heard an old man say outside the pharmacy

that has begun to resemble a Glaswegian off-licence.

They'll say – mind the gap, mind the gap

as they platform learned incredulity in the Academies,

mind the gap, between the Rich, between

the rich and the poor, like it matters anymore.

Out of this, what did the soldier's wife get?

Nothing, nothing but domestic scorn and majestic elegy

permanently disappointed needing nothing from no one

constantly making affirmations for the better,

 for us all.

Everybody knew the grave digger, we were at school

and as we grew older the architecture grew smaller

even in this town the holes remained the same.

Walking the tarmac path on acorns

is a tricky sport and

tall oaks from small acorns grow.

The girl interrupted has evidence

for the multilateral Aid Review

That speciality in learning from influence,

fucked

a daily global meditation on co-dependency.

Here is a herd of cows coming in from the cowshed

for the milking.

We're all dressing up for war

and we're sick of the indigenous population

where the country people work to grow crops.

And on Market Day many people set off

for the market town.

For hundreds of years now

country people have come to the Market Town.

And all the happy merchants bidding for their blood.

All Told.

#6.

Rise like righteous Oaks.

Never, never, never

Never, never.

All told.

#7.

The Colonic.

In the days of the eclipses –

here the eclipse alludes to the seizure of time

historical recurrence and para llel worlds.

In the gap, we were looking

for an equality of cultural prejudice.

You black people come, sit and we'll sing together,

about how difficult it has been, a parity of oppression.

From a new vantage point on the hill

a sort of homogenous particle accelerator.

Eclipses are also commonly understood

to be harbingers of change, and fittingly it will evolve

like our orchid roots bound

to the branch of a tree, cleaving.

This work presents a parallel universe,

after philosophical truth in a time where

truth is elusive, if it exists at all.

The texts suggest that reality

is an ever – changing concept

constantly revised and corrected

waiting for words to dry

from a bi-polar ink cartridge

prioritising material experience over language

as a way of learning and understanding.

Let us all listen to the leader, our leader

in the name of God I would like to salute the people.

Your performance was concerned with subtle

interventions

in time and space, silence waiting

and paying attention

to the present moment.

We never know what's going to happen

where visible objects with a secret depth

appear to reveal a kind of irrational truth.

We led the liberation to free the people

we will put two fingers in the eyes

of the defiers, for the people.

She was presented as a martyr,

victim and troublemaker

they championed and vilified her.

Making dreams of energy come true

with discussions about harnessing

non-commercial energy in art

to the creation of history and memoir through culture.

But who's manipulating who here

Those accidental drips of paint, in the studio.

How we laughed, knowing we'd paid good money

to see tin-foil on the gallery floor.

We laughed so much.

Today's experience-economy, in which shopping

is no longer about buying Things

but a Whole Retail experience.

Oh, The Leisure Sphere.

When you want to control the protest

what do you do? The state has a responsibility no?

The word 'supplicant' goes

back to the meaning of someone

who prays on your behalf;

a petitioner, a substitute

a stand-in, for something else.

Micro- sounds, such as the discarded lighter,

whose electro-magnetic spring, amplified

by contact microphones, produces harmonic

overtones.

Ah, the aesthetics of persuasion.

I liked the idea then, of a bunch of guys

sitting around a table

pondering these issues in a corporate environment.

Investigating alchemical and metaphysical

transformations of ideas

actions and materials, involving elements

of surprise and risk.

A kind of professional tomb –

a four-sided way of making theatre.

Drunk beetles in a fresh dandelion head.

Watching, we inhabit two worlds

that of fiction, that of fact.

Their union is curiously provocative

suggesting the cultural value of all iconic artefacts

as things gathered along the corridors of his and her story.

They speak of lost crafts and excavations

of memory, using rhythm and repetition

layering, juxtaposition, inversion, elaboration

stresses and pauses, architecture.

Made in winged Californian think-tanks

on the subject of political rhetoric in the global-value-chain.

 A device for crowd control,

The narrow structures through which

cattle are led to the slaughter in abattoirs.

We are the richest poor people in the world.

We have these stories to tell us so.

All Told.

All Told is a libretto for an anti-film in seven parts.

The film can only be watched

and listened to with your open mind

then, if you like, you too

can make up your mind.

We never tell truly

and Truly we are never Told.

Brand by Viktor Khoklenko

Printed in Great Britain
by Amazon

86148050R00031